THE DARKNESS WITHIN

My Journey to a New Life

the Darkness Within

my journey to a new life

michele gmitrowski

> *The illustration across from the title page was created for the author by her husband, Ted Gmitrowski. It is from a photo he took of her and depicts her inner struggle.*

Author's Note: The stories in this book reflect the author's recollection of events. Some names, locations, and identifying characteristics have been changed to protect the privacy of those depicted. Dialogue has been re-created from memory. Some names, locations, and identifying characteristics have been changed to protect the privacy of those depicted.

Copyright © 2018–2021 by Michele Gmitrowski

Edited by Andrew Durkin | Inkwater.com
Cover and interior design by Masha Shubin | Inkwater.com
Cover Artwork: Storm Clouds © Chutternsap (Unsplash.com); Wind, Waves, and Hair © Yoann Boyer (Unsplash.com); Spider Webs © Cattallina (BigStock.com).

All rights reserved. No part of this book may be reproduced or transmitted in any form or by any means whatsoever, including photocopying, recording or by any information storage and retrieval system, without written permission from the publisher and/or author.

ISBN-13 978-1-7772867-4-3

1 3 5 7 9 10 8 6 4 2

I dedicate this book to my sister Patsy, who passed away so suddenly . . . I will always miss you.

My name is Michele, and I suffer with a chemical imbalance of the brain—also known as clinical depression. I have posttraumatic stress disorder and borderline personality disorder. I was twenty-six years old when the story you are about to read began. At that time I just thought I was "crazy," as that's what people labeled anyone like me.

It all started in 1996—I believe it was springtime. After work, I was getting a ride home on the QEW from Toronto, when all of a sudden I decided to open the door while the car was going 120 kilometers an hour, and I tried to jump out. If it weren't for Sally, who was driving the car, I probably wouldn't be here today. She grabbed me and pulled me back in.

I cried as I was asked, "Why did you do that?" I had no explanation for it. That night I was taken to the hospital to speak to a psychiatrist who was in the emergency unit, who decided that I was to be admitted that evening. I was put in what they call the "A" ward of the psychiatric floor of the hospital. This "A" ward of the psychiatric floor was for the severe cases, and I had to stay there at least overnight, while they decided where I should be. That night I was left behind closed doors and felt extremely lost. It wasn't a ward you could walk in and out of; it was more like a prison for the mentally insane.

That night I woke up scared and alone, finding that a patient had wandered into my room and wound herself around the curtains by the window. I felt extremely scared, as this was the first time I'd ever experienced anything like this, or had ever been admitted into a psychiatric ward. A nurse came in and guided the girl out of the room, putting my mind at ease for that night. Needless to say, I didn't get any sleep that night, as I was afraid of the people I might be exposed to in the "A" ward.

The next day I was relieved to hear that I was going to the "B" Ward of the psychiatric floor, where all of the patients dealing with mental health problems were admitted. There I was assigned a psychiatrist, whose name was Dr. Alan. After he spoke with me, I was taken into a room by a nurse and asked many questions, which confused me quite a bit as at this time. I really didn't know what was going on or why I was there. But this was going to be the beginning of a very long journey for me, and I wasn't even aware of it.

I glared out the window with an expression so cold it would send a chill up your spine just to stand beside me. My face looked faded and dull, as though I hadn't seen the light of day in years—but really it had been three weeks since my admission into that horrid institution. The emotion I had once been able to express had vanished once again, and was deep in my soul or tucked away in that solitary darkness that haunted me day after day. I'd been sitting there for forty-five minutes with my sister, Paton. We said nothing to each other—she just kept trying to understand where I really was when she saw that expression on my face. I didn't believe she would ever know, as I just isolated myself in my catacomb.

I heard the screeching of the supper trolley down the hall, along with that ghastly odor from the trays, which clearly identified them as being from the hospital kitchen. All of a sudden the other patients slowly drifted out of their rooms, almost zombielike.

Paton and I were close—best friends. "Come on, Michele," she said, trying hard to be enthusiastic. "You really should eat something. You haven't touched any food all day. Let's try this time. Okay?"

Once again there was that dreadful silence. "Please, Michele, please . . ."

I turned to Paton very slowly, and with a soft tremulous voice replied, very reluctantly, "Okay, Paton." I thought it might be best for me to get out of my room for a while, so she suggested I sit with the other patients in the dining room—if you could call it that—rather than carrying a tray to my room, as I had been doing for a while now.

I was so very frail, and Paton really hated the medication I was on, as at times I could barely keep my head up. Paton took me by the arm as I stood up from the table and slowly walked down the hall to the dining room.

I said, "Hi" to Danny as he fumbled through the trays on the supper trolley to see if he could find his tray. Danny was schizophrenic. I never really knew how to take him, but funnily enough, it didn't bother me a bit that he was so strange.

While we searched for my supper tray, there was a sudden uproar at the other end of the dining room. "Get the hell out of my seat, bitch!" I couldn't believe it, but Danny was doing all that yelling—even though he had just calmly greeted me a minute ago.

"Sit down and shut up!" replied the rather thin-looking woman he was yelling at. She was a patient, too, and her face was covered with large boil-like spots.

"Get the hell out of my seat, bitch—didn't you hear me?" Danny said again. By this time he sounded quite violent. "Do you want your fucking block knocked off?"

By now I didn't know how much more of this I could take. Paton felt sorry for me; she said, "How the hell do you cope in here?" She grabbed my tray for me and carried it to my assigned table, sitting me down very carefully. Paton then pulled up an extra chair so that she could sit beside me in order to encourage me to eat. I looked so sad and empty, but she knew there wasn't anything she could do to make it better. She just wanted me to feel that she was close.

I began sipping the soup with Paton's help. Just as she thought she was getting somewhere with me, I heard, "Okay, people, it's time for your supper meds." It was as though the Gestapo had invaded the dining area. I turned to Paton and quietly said, "Jan is my nurse today. She's the fat one, and she's not very nice at all."

"Don't worry," Paton said, quite authoritatively. "I'm here and I won't let her bother you." And here Nurse Jan came—just as I described, but twice as boisterous. She turned to me and said, "It's about time you ate something, instead of spending time in your room glaring out the window, don't you think?" While saying this, she handed me a small cup of water and a cup full of various pills. Paton did not know what the purpose of the various pills was, and this disturbed her, but I took them as I was told.

As far as the supper went, it stopped after the soup and a sip of milk. It was always very uncomfortable being in the dining area—half the patients didn't even know where they were. Some ate as though they had never seen food before. Others simply sat there with their eyes glassy as ice, filled with tears which they wanted so much to release, but they just didn't know how. Paton never wanted to force me to sit in these surroundings for any longer than I had to, so she helped me up, and I slightly toppled over to one side, due to the effects of the medication. We gradually made our way back to my room, where I seemed to become more content.

There was nothing to look at out of the window, as it had gotten dark outside and time was passing rapidly. Paton explained to me that she had to shut the curtains now—that really seemed to upset me. Paton tried to comfort me little, knowing that she had to go home shortly, and told me that she would brush my hair. She could see that I seemed to like that idea, so she sat on the bed beside me and said, "Do you remember when we were little girls, and we played hairdresser?" Paton then began to brush my hair—which was long, but seemed to have lost all its life. "Do you remember how much you liked it when it was your turn to be the customer?" she said. "You said how special it made you feel. We did that for hours, and then we did our dolls' hair—do you remember, Michele?" She gave me a hug as she told these stories to me; I had tears in my eyes, but I wouldn't cry.

"Why don't we wash your face?" she said. "It will make you feel that much better." So we did. The room had a certain glacial feeling to it; Paton wanted to bring in some cheerful pictures for me, as she wasn't sure how long I had to be in this damned place. Paton helped me put on my night dress. I always liked nice things, so she made sure to bring one of the pretty ones from home. I looked so helpless, just like the little girl she once knew—except I was now thirty-five years old. But how much she wanted to comfort me! I said that I didn't want to go anywhere, so she didn't force me and helped to tuck me into bed. It was so close to 8:30 p.m. now, and visiting hours would be over soon. Paton stroked my head for a while as I lay there.

"Michele," she said. "You've got to *want* to get better. I love you very much—we all do. Please don't give up on life this way—get strong, fight it. You know you can."

"*Visiting hours are now over,*" came a voice over the PA system. By the ear-splitting sound of it, I could swear it was the voice of Nurse Jan. Paton gave me a kiss and a hug. "I'll be back sometime tomorrow, okay?" she said. "Please take care—just think and believe how much you're loved. I really love you." I know it was hard for Paton to see me like this; I was the baby in the family. Her throat tightened as she left. She was trying very hard not to cry in front of me. She left, and I tried hard not to turn back.

I had begun to relax and close my eyes, when I was disturbed by a sudden glare of light in my face. It was Jan, of course—the "curse of the nurses." "It's time for your bedtime meds," she said. "I've been looking all over the place for you. Why aren't you in the lounge with the others?"

I sat up, slowly. "I didn't feel like it. I'm not really feeling too well."

"How do you expect to get better by just staying in here?" she replied. "You won't get any sympathy around here, you know!" I took my meds, and as I lay down, whispered under my breath, "Bitch! I hate you." Jan just pranced out of there. I was glad to see her go. I closed my eyes once again, and with the sounds of the hospital phones ringing, and people talking in the hall, I finally fell asleep.

At 5:00 a.m., there was a slight knock on the door, and once again a flashlight shining in my face. I wiped the sleep from my eyes to see who it was. "I'm just here to take some blood, love." This of course was one of the usual routines, and certainly not a great way to begin the morning—but at least it wasn't

Nurse Jan. Anyway, it didn't take long, and I was able to roll over again to try and get back to sleep.

At 7:00 a.m. it was time to get up. The daily routine was to try and get to one of the two showers before anyone else did. While I waited there, with a towel and my clothes in hand, there was an announcement over the PA—obviously for the nurses. It was the kind of announcement nobody liked to hear—a "red alert," which meant a patient was hurt, dying, or trying to escape from the ward.

As I waited for a shower, one of the nurses came running out, saying, "Has anyone seen Danny? Does anyone know where he is? He's not in his room or in the dining area. Does anyone know anything?" One of the patients blurted out, "All we know is that we've been waiting for this damned shower for ages. Who the hell is in there, anyway? Can't you tell them to hurry up and get out?"

The nurse began to bang on the door. "There's a line up out here—hurry up! Who's in there, anyway? What are you doing?" All that could be heard was the shower water running—but other than that there was dead silence. I, along with the others, suddenly all stood back against the wall, while the nurse ran to get the key. There was a sudden stillness in the air. "I'm coming in," the nurse said once she had returned, and unlocked the door. "Oh my god—get help! Quick, hurry!"

Some of the other patients just couldn't wait

to look over the nurse's shoulder, to see what had happened. I just froze, and felt so terribly alone and terrified. Someone yelled out, "It's Danny! It's Danny—there's blood and everything!"

Suddenly a doctor and two other nurses came running toward us. "Everyone move away, clear the area." They went into the shower area, where Danny was. He was later carried out on a stretcher, with his face covered. Jonathan, one of the other patients, who often spoke to me, turned to me and said, "Did you hear? He killed himself. Funny thing though—the poor bastard probably wasn't aware of what the hell he was doing, or who the fuck he was."

I blankly looked at him, not fully understanding what he meant. Then I hugged myself and walked back to my room. The ward seemed in total chaos. Some patients were crying, and others had the same blank expression I had—but no one was able to offer consolation.

At breakfast, I went to the dining area, but only to pick my breakfast tray off the trolley, and return with it to my room. That awful nurse, Jan, wasn't in today, so Sue was my nurse for the day. She was always very nice to me. While in my room, attempting to eat some of that stuff they called breakfast, I faced the window once again. The sun was shining outside. It was actually the first few days of summer weather. You could feel the warmth of the sun off the window. I thought to myself how sad it was that Danny had killed himself. It just didn't seem fair that I was sitting there in my room, still able to enjoy the sunlight. But it gave me a sudden inner strength—it made me *want* to be alive.

After breakfast, rather than just lying down on my bed, as I had been doing recently, I decided to get dressed, do my hair, and even apply a little makeup. While I was doing this, there was a knock on my door. It was my family doctor, Dr. Ivan. He dropped in quite often on those of his patients who had been admitted into the hospital—just to talk to them and have them share any concerns they may have.

"Hello, Michele," he said, as he came and sat beside me on the bed. "And how are you feeling today?"

"I'm not feeling all that good today, Dr. Ivan, but as you can see I'm making a big effort today to try and make myself feel as though I'm alive." I tried to say it with a bit of enthusiasm.

"Well, keep up the good work, and keep your chin up, okay?" Dr. Ivan said, as he smiled cheerfully at me, tapping me on my back as though he were an old uncle of mine. Actually, he had been my doctor since I was seventeen, and he basically knew everything about me. I felt comfortable whenever he took the time to visit me—even if it was just for a while.

Suddenly there was a knock on the door. It was my roommate, Moira, a recovering anorexic. "It's your sister on the phone," she asked. "Can you take it?"

"Yes," I said. "I'll be right there—don't hang up." I hurried out of the room to the phone (all the phones were pay phones, and located in the dining room). A patient of the ward wasn't allowed to have a phone in their room, due to the cord, which could be used in a suicide attempt. Thus you could never really speak privately there—other patients often tried to listen in on your conversation. I took the phone and cupped my hand over the mouthpiece, giving myself the best protection I could.

"Hi, Paton!" I said, sounding very anxious.

"Are you okay, Michele?" she asked. "Did I wake you?"

Paton seemed quite worried that something was wrong with me. "No, you didn't wake me," I said. "Actually, would you believe that I'm dressed and wearing some makeup? And Dr. Ivan came to see me and made me feel quite good. And, oh—remember Danny? Well . . . well . . ." I stalled.

"What is it?" she said. "Tell me, and I'll talk to the nurse about him. Are you okay?"

"Danny killed himself in the shower this morning," I said. "He always tried to talk to me, Paton, and I never really took the time to listen. I really think that was all he needed—a friend to listen." There was a sudden silence on the phone. I began to cry, trying to hide my tears from the other patients in the dining room, and putting my hand on my forehead.

"Oh no," Paton said. "I'm so sorry, Michele. Don't start feeling guilty. I'm sure he knew it was difficult for you to talk to him. He'd been in that hospital much longer than you. He was sick, Michele—that's all. Please don't blame yourself. Look, I'll be dropping by at lunchtime to see you, okay? Will you be alright until I get there?"

"I'll be okay—I just want to get out of this damned place. I've just had enough. I don't want to end up like Danny." I felt very desperate at this point.

"You won't end up like Danny," she replied. "I won't let you. I'll see you at lunchtime, all right? Bye." I put the phone down. Feeling extremely lonely, I slowly walked back to my room.

I look back at those days, and it seems surreal. But that was just a taste of what I went through. The group therapy I had there brought up everything from my past—like my dad's passing from a heart attack at the age of fifty-four, and the fact that I didn't get to say goodbye to him, and the guilt I feel to this day. When we lived in India, I had been sexually abused. I was three at the time—I can see where it happened and what was done to me, but I can never see the face of the person. I mean, who do you tell when you're that young? All I know (from my mum) is that I was a miserable child back then. She didn't know why, and when she found out during my stay at the hospital, she asked, "Why didn't you tell me?" That wasn't easy for me to do back then—talking to my mum wasn't easy.

I also found out that at the age of five, when we were living in England with some people we knew, a young girl sexually abused me. What did I know? To me, it was a game. She called it "house." There was a door under the stairs where was a small space, enough to play. I'm sure I'm not the only child who went through that.

After a few more group therapy sessions, I spoke of more of the abuse that had happened to me. At the age of seven, I was followed by an old man from school—again, this was when we lived in England. When I stopped at a store called Woolworth's, he followed me in, and rubbed himself against me sexually. I didn't really know what he was doing, but it didn't feel right. All I can remember is not telling anyone, and knowing it was wrong. I ran out of that store as fast as I could, only to find that he was still following me. I was so scared that I don't really know how I made it home. Again, I told nobody. I didn't think my mum would believe me, because she used to tell me that I was so dramatic, and that I liked to tell stories. I was only seven years old—the youngest of three girls in our family—and kept that all inside.

I remember when we lived in England. We had our own house in London. I was sitting with my Nana one time, and a sudden fear of death came over me. I was only seven years old, and I began to cry, not really knowing why. She asked what was wrong, but I really didn't know what to say, or how to explain it. I also had recurring dreams back then; one involved the sky being spider webs, and I would feel trapped; the other was of a bowling alley, with a ball that would roll but never get to the pins. I didn't even know what a bowling alley was until I got older. These lasted quite a few years, and I had no idea what they meant at the time.

Now I don't mean to jump back in my story to my time at the hospital, but it's important at this point of my story. By the time I was about twenty-nine or thirty years old, I had been in and out of that damned hospital six or seven times, for weeks at a time, and usually because I didn't want to live anymore. It made me wonder: was what was in my past really important? Had it made me a better person? Or was it better to just never know at all, and live in silence?

Bringing up the past—including the verbal and mental abuse—had made me feel worse about myself. I hated looking in the mirror. I didn't like myself, never mind love myself—and no, I didn't want to live anymore. Well, that particular time at the hospital, I was approached by a priest. Apparently, he wasn't assigned to one church—he travelled from place to place, including hospitals, offering help to patients who needed it.

I'm Catholic, and used to go to church regularly as a child. As I grew older, I went only on Christmas and Easter. However, during all that time, I had never gone to confession—something you're supposed to do. Somehow I skipped it, and got away with just praying on my own at night. Regardless—here was this priest, and I thought to myself, what better time to give my confession? I could do it while at the hospital, feeling the way I was. He was there for confessions, and to pray for you, and I'm really not sure what else. All I know is I was heavily sedated, as that's all that hospital ever did—I guess it meant less work for them.

Another girl and I wanted to have the same opportunity to take confession—we wanted to go together, as we knew each other and felt we needed support from each other. I weighed a little over a hundred pounds, and the other girl was larger—not that it should have made any difference when it came to this. The priest insisted we each go in separately. He wanted me to be first, behind closed doors where nobody could see. I was nervous, because I'd never done this and felt I had so much to confess. Him being a priest, I trusted him. Well when he began to speak, I couldn't believe what came out of his mouth. He told me what nice breasts I had, and what a nice figure I had. He just went on talking about my physical appearance, which I was uncomfortable with as it was. I was in absolute shock, because not once did he ask me what I'd like to confess.

When I came out of that room the other girl looked at me and asked if I was okay. But I had no words. The priest told the other girl that he didn't have time to hear her confession, but wanted to bless the both of us. To tell you the truth, I don't even know what he was saying by then—I just went with it. When he was done, he offered us a hug if we wanted, and I very quickly responded, "No." But he hugged me anyway, and rubbed himself hard against me—I could feel his penis against my body. I felt sick to my stomach, and I froze, not knowing what to say, and feeling frightened.

I didn't speak of that experience until two weeks later, when I told my family. They told the hospital, which did nothing about it. We couldn't even track this man down. My mum really wanted to—especially now, knowing what I had been through. But I told her just to leave it alone, as I was afraid of having to face this man again. Needless to say, he stole something from me that day—he stole my faith in God. I avoided churches for years, and still feel uncomfortable in them to this day.

I think that's what made it so difficult when, a few years after my dad passed away, my mum remarried a friend of the family, who lived in England, and was a priest when I was a young girl. He was actually the priest who performed my First Communion. I didn't deal with them getting married very well at all—after all, I was still dealing with the death of my dad, and still dealing with the guilt. I felt so much anger—I guess towards myself, but I took it out on the wrong people. Mum remarried a good man, really—he never expected us to call him "Dad," and was always there for us when we needed him. We were able to keep my dad's pictures up, which was comforting.

I think Mum married him mainly because she was lonely and needed companionship, because I know she still loves my dad to this day. But back then I couldn't see that. All I could see was the negative aspect rather than the positive. I couldn't see the difference it made in her life.

What is love, anyway? I'm not really sure I even knew, especially after all the abuse I had experienced. Yes, I got married, and I have two wonderful children. However, a man who was my boss, during the time of my illness, seduced me. He would listen to me talk when I needed someone to talk to—unfortunately; my husband at the time would not. At the time I don't know what it was about my boss that made me think I loved him, because I don't believe I knew what real love was. He manipulated and controlled me like I was under his spell. It's really hard to explain, but it took him breaking up my marriage and me living with him to find out what kind of monster he really was. And let me not forget to mention that he was almost twice my age.

It wasn't because he had money—I'm not a materialistic person. Besides, I knew money couldn't buy me happiness, and I made that quite clear. I blame him not only for losing my husband but also for losing my two children, who were having a hard enough time dealing with my illness as it was. I love them with all my heart—and yes, *that* love I know was real. Nothing can take away the love you have for your child.

I never realized that this man—who I'd rather not even name, as he's not worth it—was an alcoholic. Why didn't I realize this every time he took me to lunch or dinner? The drinks were always the most important thing to him, and always while at work as well. I remember coming back from lunch and obviously smelling of alcohol, but without a co-worker mentioning it to me, I wouldn't have given it much thought.

What's it like living with an alcoholic? Hell! That's all I can say—it was sheer hell, and he was controlling to a point that he scared me. I felt so alone, and I didn't know how to leave him. Every night, with alcohol on his breath, he forced me to have sex with him. I felt like I was being raped every time, and would cry quietly to myself. He also forced me to drink. I know you must be thinking nobody can *force* you to drink, but he did—it was either that or he would start a fight, or else punish me with silence for days at a time, knowing that silence was a huge trigger for me, and something I couldn't handle.

He would call me names, making me beg on hands and knees to live with him. He knew I had no way out at that time in my life. I was sick and on medication, and he took full advantage of my vulnerability and the fact that I had nobody to turn to. My family had stopped talking to me for quite a while when I was with him—and who could blame them? I didn't see it then, but I do now. All I knew was to be controlled by this man. When we would go anywhere I was like a trophy to him. But I didn't feel like a trophy—I was scared and embarrassed.

When it was my weekend with my children, and I went to see them, I never knew what I was going to come home to with this man. Was he going to sit in the dark and ignore me? Was he going to argue with me over nothing? I was always scared. We had a fridge with an icemaker, and every time I heard the clinking of cubes into his glass, I knew I was going to have a night of hell. My husband had written in a journal since he was a child, but now that journal had also become a weapon against me. He would tell me some of the horrible things he was going to write, or sometimes he would just go into his office and leave me in the silence, except when I heard the *clink* of the ice cubes hitting the glass.

I had been advised by my psychiatrist to write in a journal from the time when I was married. I did that for a while, and then I began recording my journal on cassette tapes. He had the nerve to take my journals and not only read them, but also type them out and keep them locked up along with his journal—and if I dared to say anything, it would mean punishment for me. We first lived on the thirtieth floor of a condominium building, and unfortunately during that time I was suicidal. I would cry my eyes out and grab a handful of pills, or go on the balcony. He would just shut the lights off and go to bed—he didn't give a damn. Thank God my senses got the best of me. When my children came to mind it put me back into a safe place.

Then he bought a house out in the country—I mean really *in the country*. The town consisted of just over one hundred people. There was one street, and one corner store. I was really worried about my safety, as I knew he had two rifles in the house. I don't even think they were registered. On one of his good days, I persuaded him to give the guns to a young couple who lived across the street—the husband liked to hunt. Somehow he actually listened and did just that.

Thank God my sister Paton was still very close to me. I was able to go visit her and stay over—she lived over an hour away, but it was worth getting away from the monster I was living with (I mean, what else could I call him?). One day Paton and her husband visited. They were a very open couple, and nothing really bothered them. Don't ask me why, but one day as they visited, and the monster was of course drinking—he was drinking a lot now, as he had retired early and so was home all the time—he came out naked and sat there and talked to them. Paton asked me what the hell was going on. She knew the situation I was in but couldn't help me—I had to help myself. I asked him to put some clothes on. All he did was laugh, telling me he was comfortable, and speaking for my sister and her husband, saying, "They're okay."

It was one the most uncomfortable, embarrassing moments at that house. While dressed, he would pull his penis out and play with it. It was just disgusting, and to this day I still get flashbacks of this man and what he put me through. I remember us staying at a hotel in Montreal once. Needless to say, he had two things on his mind: sex and alcohol. He would force me to do demeaning things that are really difficult to talk about. This time in Montreal, while controlling me, he pushed me on the bed, wrapping his hands around my throat to the point where I thought I was going to pass out. I was so scared—I struggled, trying to tell him to stop until he finally did. He said he was only messing around. He could have killed me that night—I could see it in his evil eyes. Even though they were blue, they seemed black at times like this.

You'd think that vacations would be something to look forward to, especially given some of the places we visited, like Australia, Tahiti, Bali, Hawaii, various cruises, etc. But I could never look forward to those vacations—I knew I would never have good memories from them. Alcohol had to be a main factor in everything we did. Sometimes during the day it was fine, but when he kept drinking through the afternoon, I knew what the evening was going to be like. It was like walking on eggshells with him all the time. How can one enjoy a vacation under those circumstances? He may as well have had a leash on me so he could walk me around, doing only what he wanted to do, and seeing only what he wanted to see. He made sure he visited every bar he could on those vacations. And yes, I was made to drink with him or else.

Living out in the country with this monster, and with only a few other houses on the street, I could have felt quite isolated. However, I was so happy that I had my Jack Russell dog, who I called Bianca. Of course, he would call her something else. He had two Burmese cats, which I also loved, and I am surprised that I was allowed to have this dog, which showed me so much love and was my companion. I loved living out in the country, and I wish I had been living out there with somebody else rather than this person. Unfortunately that wasn't my choice at the time.

I never thought I would meet anyone else for the rest of my life. I used to take Bianca for many walks. The town, as I said, was quite small: approximately one hundred people, with a U-shaped street, and houses quite spread out. Taking a walk with Bianca gave me some peace of mind—it let me get away from this man. However, I had not made any friends—but that's the story of my life. I've always found it hard to make friends, due to trust issues. If I did find a friend, that friend would be my one and only.

I would literally do anything just to be away from this man. I loved the fact that we had half an acre of land. I enjoyed cutting the grass with the riding lawn mower because I could take my mind elsewhere and feel happy. At times he would ruin that as well by coming out there with a drink in hand and suggesting we do some garden work. Of course, I always had to go along with it, and pretend that I was enjoying it. But I wasn't. I had no choice, because if

I said *no* I would have had to face the consequences, which could be quite harsh.

I spent many evenings alone, while he sat in his office, writing in his journal, which he locked away with a key. He was so secretive about his journal, locking it away with a key, and then hiding the key and making sure I knew that I would never find it. He would make it a point to let me know if he was angry—telling me he was entering something bad about me in his journal.

Actually, any time after he drank, he would find fault with anything I was doing. I have suffered with low self-esteem since I was a child, and his demeaning me just made it that much worse. His face was that of evil, filled with anger and hatred.

There came a time when I would make an excuse just to get out of the house. I would tell him I was going to the casino. It wasn't close to where we lived, but I felt safe driving alone on those dark country roads—and besides, it was worth it just to get away. Surprisingly, he didn't stop me from going. I would literally spend hours and hours there—from morning to late evening—just to be around friendly people who I could talk to and laugh with. They may have been strangers to me, but the more I went, the more I got to know them. So this was my escape—until of course I became addicted to the slots, especially after winning so many jackpots. Like many gamblers, I thought that I would win every time I went there. The money I used was my own. I would use my credit card, and when it became maxed out, I felt this sudden feeling of loss—not because of the money, but because of the loss of all the people I had met, and the happy times I had there, just being away from him.

So here I was back at the place I hated so much—stuck with this monster and knowing that now I had no place to go.

One day as I was walking Bianca, I met a woman who I believe to this day was an angel. She lived two doors down from us, in a house with her husband and three children. She called me over, and being desperate for companionship, I went over to her. She was sitting on the steps of her house and I sat beside her. Her name was May, and she knew, somehow, that I was struggling and unhappy. So we talked briefly and became friends. Her family was wonderful. She was a flight attendant and her husband a pilot. She always had a warm, welcoming face, and when I visited with them I felt safe. They attended a Baptist church in the town nearby, and invited me to join them. I was hesitant at first, but when I saw how happy they were to go there, I wanted to go as well.

It was like something I had never experienced before. When I entered this church, everyone knew each other. There were smiles on people's faces, and they had a band up where the minister was speaking. He spoke of everyday things, and did not preach in the way I was used to. When the band played, we all stood up there. People sang along with songs that did not sound like hymns, but beautiful meaningful music. We danced where we stood, clapping along. The feeling that came over me was one of acceptance, love, and happiness.

One day, when I went with May's family to church, after she started learning more of what my life was like, the minister asked people to come up front—anyone who felt they needed prayers, for whatever reason. May turned to me and said "Michele, why don't you go up there?" And I did, because I needed someone to care—I needed some hope for my life. There, people who did not even know me showed that they genuinely cared. They mentioned my name and prayed for me, surrounding me with what felt like love. I really can't explain the feeling of calm that came over me—I actually smiled.

Church became a good place for me again. After everything I had experienced in the past, and after losing my faith, I felt I was getting it back. But it was different, and enjoyable. I looked forward to going with them, and at this point didn't really care what the monster in our home thought. This was *my* time and *my* friends. He actually became jealous, and of course had to make it something dirty—saying that May and I were lesbians and how he would love to see us together. It was typical of him to try and turn my happiness around, but this time I didn't let him.

May was my friend, and when I told her what he said, she told me, "Let him think whatever he wants, he's an evil man." And she was right.

One day when I went over to May's home, she and her husband asked me if I would mind if they prayed with me. Of course I said no. They were not trying to change the person that I was, or my beliefs—they just truly cared about my well-being. They wanted to do anything and everything they could to help. May's husband Nigel even told me, "You don't need a special place to pray." He giggled. "I pray wherever I am—I just do it as if I am talking to God as a friend. You don't need to be in a church to do that." It was so true—I know because I remember my dad was like that. He would pray out loud in the car if he wanted to.

And then I began to find strength in myself—something I had never known I had. I learned how I could stand up for myself—that the monster did not own me, and that I did not have to live that way anymore. And I owed May, the angel who was sent to me, for the changes that were about to happen.

She helped me see that I was living in an unhealthy home, which I had to get out of before it damaged me any further. She helped me find out where to begin. She came with me to get legal aid from a lawyer in the next town. I qualified for it, being on disability and not married. The lawyer was there to help me know my rights, as I was living common law with this monster. She said I deserved to get something out of this awful situation. Legally, because I had now lived with him for two years, I was entitled to something if I planned on leaving him. It was a huge step for me to just make that decision, because I was so scared of being alone. He had made me feel that nobody would ever want me or love me again. Although the lawyer could not represent me in court, she could prepare me to represent myself—another big step in my life. It's not easy putting together legal documents, especially as I was in such a dark place in my life. But I had to find it in me to do so.

Needless to say, I found the strength and served that monster with the papers. Of course he found the most expensive lawyer he could to fight me, though I had nobody but myself to represent me in court.

I will save you all the details—suffice it to say that after that I was treated worse than ever. But I had to stay there—if I had left I would not have had a case against him.

When it came to the big day in court, May came with me as support. That was what I really needed at this time. I was scared even though I was in a courtroom full of people. Yes I had been through a similar experience when I divorced my ex-husband; however, back then, when the monster supposedly "cared" about me, he paid for the lawyer. I was very ill at that time, and having that aid was very helpful, even though it came from him. Of course, it was a selfish move on his part, as he wanted me all to himself, and I was blind to that fact at the time.

I was already in the courtroom with May, when we saw the monster arrive with his lawyer. He looked over at me with an evil smirk. A few cases went up before mine, so I was very on edge, and then I heard my name called. I provided the judge with all kinds of exhibits along with my legal papers to prove that this monster has looked upon me and displayed me to everyone as his wife. I felt I needed as much evidence as I could get to prove my case against him. Once I was done, the judge dismissed me with thanks, and seemed pleased at how I had put my papers together, and also how I had provided him with plenty of background information.

Now it was the monster's turn. His lawyer went up to defend him until the judge asked to speak with the monster himself. He had the nerve to say that I was merely a roommate who stayed at the house. He dismissed and lied about everything he had done—everything he had said to me or referred to me as. He was soon put in his place, when the judge produced several cards I had saved from past birthdays and Christmases. He asked, "It clearly states here 'to my wife' in all these cards—why would you say now that she was only a roommate?" Finally the monster had nothing to say. He looked at his lawyer and they were caught in a lie.

I won my case. He had to provide me a certain amount of money (not that this was important to me, but I did deserve it). It was nothing compared to what his wife was still getting every month. The only regret I had was that I did not bring up the threats he made on my life, the time the police came to the house, etc. I think those things were important, but I guess I just wanted out and was trying to do everything the way I thought I was supposed to.

As the days passed, it was most uncomfortable, but I had no reason to explain myself to him for anything anymore. One day I came to the house and began calling my dog. "Bianca," I said. "It's Mummy, where are you?" And then he spoke words I did not expect to hear. "I gave her away to someone, and she'll be fine," he said, aggressively. My eyes filled with tears. He had given away my companion, who had given me so much comfort in that house during the toughest of times. If it weren't for her and our walks I would have never met May, and never left him.

I asked him why, but all he said was that she would be fine, and provided me with an address and phone number of the person who had taken her. She was far away now. What kind of a person does something like that? That's all he ever did—hurt me in every way possible. But giving Bianca away was just too much. It was like taking away my child. I was quite distraught, with only May to comfort me. I really missed Bianca, and now there was a large void.

May helped me look for an apartment I could afford, close to where she lived. We finally found a very small basement apartment of a house where I felt I would be safe. It would be mine. There was no room to swing a cat in there, never mind have anyone over. I did have my children visit me, and they made me feel that it was a very nice place—especially during Christmas, when I had a tree that was twelve inches tall. We just laughed about it.

The times I spent there alone—which was most of the time, because I was on permanent disability at this time—were lonely, I have to admit. But I tried to make it as warm as possible. After all, I only had the space of not even half of that basement. But I knew it was only temporary. At least I didn't have to worry about what I was coming home to, or be terrified when I heard that monster pour himself a drink. He was out of my life for good now.

I used to spend some nights over at my sister Paton's place. We had fun, laughing at every little thing, and enjoying each other's company. She had suggested that I put in an application at her apartment building—it was a subsidized building, and with me being on disability my rent would be much lower than what I was paying at my current place. I guess luck was on my side—I had only lived in this small basement apartment for seven months, but the landlords were a nice couple, and understood why I had to break the lease. I got a nice two-bedroom apartment on the sixth floor, with a balcony. I could see the lake. The place was mine.

I had actually started going out by myself during the time I spent there, as my niece, Paton's daughter, used to be a waitress at a bar and encouraged me to come out. I surprised myself when I did—I guess I felt safe because I knew she was there. It was the start of a new life for me, and I was at a stage in my life I never thought I would reach.

Well, moving day came, and I knew I was going to be living about an hour away from May, who had been such a wonderful, kind, and caring friend. I knew she would always be there for me. I did not have much to move, as I only took what was mine from that monster. I wouldn't have wanted anything of his, as I did not want any reminders of all he had put me through. Sadly, I had triggers—something I could not control—because of what he had put me through. I now had to learn how to deal with them.

I rented a small van—and when I say small, I mean really small. I just about got everything I had into it. The movers really took their time, but this was the only choice I had at the time. To top it off, it was a rainy day, but I was getting a place in my sister's building and was looking forward to it.

I had never had an actual apartment of my own. Once everything was in its place, I have to admit, it suddenly seemed so big and empty. I also have to admit that the first night was the hardest, since I wasn't used to this. But I knew that Paton was on the main floor. I didn't want to take advantage and show up at Paton's place every day, so I tried to become independent—which was scary for me, but I knew I had to do it. My niece had now moved to another bar, which was in the same town I was living in. It was an Irish bar, which was really nice. It had a band a couple of nights a week, and dancing. I used to go there on Friday and Saturday nights, and would sit at the bar because the bartenders knew me, since my niece worked there. I felt safe, and they would make sure I got a taxi home, especially on the days when my niece was not working.

Michele Gmitrowski

I had figured that I had dealt with all the monsters in my life by now. But I guess I was wrong. I was quite naïve, trusting everyone and feeling nobody could hurt me. When I went to the ladies' room at this bar I would ask the bartender to watch my drink, as I had heard stories of people getting their drinks drugged.

One night I was talking to a pretty good-looking, much younger guy, who I had seen there before. I excused myself to go to the ladies' room. He was still there when I got back, and so was my beer. He was getting a little too familiar with me, and I didn't warm up to him, so he left rather suddenly. I began to feel really sleepy, so one of the bartenders, who had obviously seen people who had their drinks drugged before, told me to come to sit closer to where the waitresses were at the bar. I was basically sleeping at the bar, only to find out much later that I had been drugged. That same guy had done it to one of the women bouncers who worked there.

This was a whole new chapter in my life, and I knew I had to be careful. At the same time, I felt it was my turn to have a life, and live it to the fullest. I was extra cautious after this incident—at this and any other bar I went to. You could say I became rather promiscuous and carried away with the freedom I now had—something I had never done in the past, since I had married young and had children quite soon after. Many obviously younger guys enjoyed my company, and I enjoyed theirs. One thing would lead to another—and the pattern would repeat itself. I wasn't looking for another relationship—I wanted to have fun. At the same time, I tried to be as ladylike as possible, as I didn't want to appear cheap.

I made quite a few acquaintances during this time—all of whom were basically my son's age. Looking back, I think it was much better than being with someone who was twice my age, like the monster in my life had been. I briefly dated a few of these younger acquaintances, but like I said, I wasn't looking for anything serious. One night at the bar, when my niece was not working, one of her friends, a guy, who I also knew, called me over to a table. He and two other guys were there, and one of them was closer to my age. They told me that it was his birthday, and asked if I wanted to celebrate with them. Of course, I said yes.

I didn't realize that this celebration meant leaving my safe place—the bar—and going to this older guy's house with the other two. We lived close to a famous golf course, and beside this were some massive homes. This man lived in one of them. Apparently he had children and wasn't married—thus he was not my cup of tea—but I was there merely to help celebrate his birthday. Once we were in the house, which was quite impressive, my niece's friend gave me a shot. We were all going to cheer for this guy's

The Darkness Within

birthday. I literally had a sip, and remember nothing after that.

I woke up with this man basically raping me. I had been unconscious and now my arm hurt. When I looked over to see why, I discovered that somehow during the time I was unconscious, my arm got stuck in a bar stool from the night before—part of the stool had been sawed off and the rest was left on my arm. To think that all this was done just so this man could have his way with me. When I felt more alert, I asked, "Where am I, what are you doing, and where are my clothes?" Quickly, he got up and gave a lame apology. I don't know if the drugs were still in my system, because I didn't find it strange that I had been left there, with the back of a bar stool stuck to my arm, which was swollen by now. This man had some sense—enough to drive me in his fancy red Ferrari to the hospital, as my arm was obviously not okay. He said he would wait—and I really don't know what happened then. My mind was still a blur. When asked at the hospital how this happened I didn't know what to say. I didn't even think about telling them that the man sitting in the waiting area did this to me and raped me. I had no recollection of what had happened during the time I had been drugged the night before, so I didn't know how I got my arm stuck in this barstool the way it was. I was just in so much pain by now that I wanted the stool off my arm. The doctor literally had to wheel a gurney over to the area where the maintenance guys worked and literally sawed this off my arm, which was quite swollen at this point.

My arm was put in a cast. I'm not sure why, but I accepted a ride home from this man and never ever saw him again. It was only later, when my daughter was visiting and I was in the car with her, that I spoke out about it. I told her I was raped as we drove past the area where this man lived.

Here I thought I had seen all the monsters in my life, only to come across another, after trusting a person I was with. My niece's friend avoided me after that day, and I wanted nothing to do with him for setting that up and drugging me to a point where I could have died, given all the medication I was on. Needless to say, it was a huge wake-up call. I became a little less open with people. I decided to continue taking part in karaoke with some of the people I knew at the bar, as it was something I enjoyed. I began having fun, trying very hard to forget.

I now realized that the world is a scary place. I had been a victim one too many times. I went back to the Irish pub—nobody there had harmed me. As I said, I never saw my niece's friend again after that. I went back to sitting at the bar, many times alone, and just watching everyone. I guess I felt I had created a bit of a cocoon for myself once again—but I *had* to, for my own safety.

I sat at the same spot at the bar every time I was there. When I looked over across the bar, I saw the sweet, kind face of a guy I didn't know. He just smiled. For the next two weeks we sat at our spots and just smiled. Once when I was coming out of the ladies' room, we bumped into each other. I surprised myself when I said, "I was hoping to bump into you." He smiled and said the same thing, told me his name was Ted, and invited me to come and meet his friends. He was soft-spoken and felt like such a kind person—something I hadn't experienced in a while. I got to know his friends, and he asked me over to his house, which he shared with a girl. He rented the upstairs and she rented the downstairs.

She was upstairs more than I would have expected, but I guess they were friends, so I accepted that.

We became a couple. He was nine years younger than me, but that didn't bother me, as he was mature, and worked for a major newspaper downtown. Ted's roommate also worked there. I guess I wondered about them, to be honest. I asked him if there was anything between them, as we shared everything about each other. He told me no, they were just friends. But she was a little too touchy-feely with him—more than I would have liked.

Yes, he was a very special person. I felt blessed to have him in my life, and my children were also very happy for me, as well as the rest of my family. He would spend a few nights at my place, and then I would spend a few nights at his.

At times I felt very uncomfortable, as his roommate would always be there with us—almost like she had to take away that special time from us, or was trying to make me jealous. Well, actually, she *did* make me jealous, in the way she spoke to him, and because of her familiarity and the fact that they worked and commuted together. Was this just me feeling insecure, or was there something he wasn't telling me? Or was it that she had imagined a different scenario with him, and he just took it as friendship? Maybe I was overthinking, but after all I had been through, I felt threatened by her, and he could not understand why. I did bring it up when we had been together for a while. Ted just could not see what I was seeing.

Well, I considered myself blessed with a wonderful man, and tried focusing on that, as I never thought I'd ever find one again, or ever be loved by one again. But things changed suddenly, and when I least expected it. It happened during a party she had planned for all their (mostly her) friends. I had just come over, and barely had a chance to say hello to everyone, when she handed me a drink. I began feeling ill—like I was going to pass out. I thought to myself, *Is this really happening?* And of course all this took place as he was also going around and greeting everyone. So he had no idea what I was going through. Needless to say, I didn't know many people there. When he found out how I was feeling, he became concerned. He knew I was on medication, and asked if I wanted to lie down.

Ted's roommate suggested that I go down lay in her bed, as everyone was upstairs. At this point, I just need to get to a bed, because I didn't know what was happening to me. Ted asked if I wanted him to stay, and I said no, it's okay. I passed out and was left downstairs after that. When I came to, I slowly made my way upstairs; only to find out that hours had gone by. Everyone had left, and she and another girlfriend of theirs were sitting on either side of Ted—a little too comfy for my liking. I knew what it felt like to be drugged, since it had happened before. I believed she had done this to me deliberately. She said, with a big smile on her stupid face, "How are you feeling? Are you okay?" I just responded that I wasn't feeling well and I was not sure what had happened.

I stayed there that night with Ted. The next morning, when she wasn't around, I brought this up to him, telling him what I believed had happened. He kept saying she wouldn't do that—which made me more and more angry and upset, as I felt Ted wasn't standing up for me. It had been a while since I felt like I was losing someone, and a while since my last suicide attempt. Crying, I got a bottle of my pills and told him I could not understand why he didn't believe me, or why he kept defending her. Then I took the bottle of pills.

He called 911 right away, and an ambulance came and took me to the hospital. I was okay, but they wanted to admit me. I remember the doctor coming in. I actually begged him to let me leave that night. I told the doctor I would be okay. Surprisingly, he allowed me to leave. It was the first time I had seen Ted—the man I loved so much—actually cry. I realized that I had hurt him, when actually I wasn't angry with him at all, I was angry with his roommate.

The next day, when Ted went to work, I stayed at his place. Unfortunately, his roommate was there, and I really didn't want anything to do with her. She was surprised that we had gone to the hospital, as she did not know everything that had taken place because she had been at work. Strangely enough, she started to spend more time downstairs at her own place after that night. And Ted and I started spending more time together at my place after that incident. Was my life going to take a wrong turn again, or would it lead somewhere happy?

I have always felt that I don't really deserve a happy life after everything I have been through. I question anything good that happens in my life because I feel like I am being tested, or that God is punishing me for anything I have done wrong in my past. But do I deserve to feel that I am constantly being punished? To this day I ask myself this question. I guess I will never see myself as others do.

Anyway, I know I am kind of drifting off the path here with my thoughts, so let me get back to what I was talking about.

This was a good man who I had finally found—or should I say, who found me. We shared everything that had happened to us in our lives, down to the details you would not normally tell anyone. We discussed living together even after everything that had taken place with me. I thought that would have scared him away. He agreed that financially it would be a great idea. Ted also said that he didn't want to live anymore with the woman who had caused so much distress.

We began looking for places, and went to check them out, until finally we came across a woman who owned several homes and rented them out. The price was perfect. She was quite a nice person, and it would feel like our own home—which to me was amazing, as I was beginning to feel a little more secure by this time. Because of my medication, I knew the rest of my life would be a rollercoaster, but I felt I had come a long way.

It was time to start a new chapter in my life, with someone who loved me as much as I loved him. We moved into the house, which was on a pleasant street, and not far from my sister. That made me happy. It had a nice backyard, was convenient for him to get to the highway, and close to stores. Suddenly, I felt calm. Because I was now on permanent disability, I was home a lot. When Ted left for work, I really felt a void, so I decided to do some volunteer work at the YMCA. It was another big step for me, as I had found it hard to do anything after being off work since 1996. The whole idea of meeting new people and doing new things felt scary, but as time went on, it gave me a purpose, and made me feel good. I even started to go to one of the workout classes; I tried to get involved as much as my mind and body would allow me to.

Being on medication was tough, especially after all the different ones I had been on. However, I knew it was necessary. I had a good psychiatrist who made sure I was put on the ones that would not make me numb to feelings, like some of them do. I also knew that if I came off the medication, it could cause serious effects. I would end up in the hospital again—a place I never wanted to be, especially for this. I used to go for sessions with my psychiatrist. I thought to myself, "I really don't have anything negative to talk about this session." But it was strange—as I spoke with him I usually filled that hour with no problem.

I remember the psychiatrist from the hospital I was at—during his sessions he was running a damned travel agency, and would take calls during my time with him. Also, he would use me as a guinea pig—trying all kinds of medication on me, regardless of the effects. And when a certain medication didn't work, he asked me to return it to him. I found out later that he gave it to other patients. I heard a few years later that he had been sued, because he should not have been redistributing medication that way. These are the risks people like me take when admitted to a hospital—you really have no choice when you're there. After having this bad experience with my psychiatrist, it was nice to find out that at least I was able to register with another psychiatrist. If I was not comfortable with the one I chose, I could find someone else. That's one benefit of living in Canada—we have good health coverage. Thank God it covers psychiatrists and therapists—too bad not enough people use them when they should.

One night when I least expected it, and when we were both in our pajamas at home, it happened—the man I loved got down on one knee and proposed to me. I was in shock, and of course I cried. When did I not? That's not always a bad thing. He had actually asked my mum for her blessing as well—something else I had no idea he would do. I felt so happy.

We had been in that house for about a year. During that time we had a cat, and got another Jack Russell. That also made me very happy. Her name was Madison, and she was the sweetest little puppy. My whole family was so happy to hear that Ted and I were engaged. They all seemed to love him, too—I mean, how could you not? Ted was the most soft-spoken, gentle person I had ever met. I honestly felt that I had been blessed, and that an angel had sent him to me.

I had not met Ted's parents or his family yet, so we booked a trip to Manitoba. He lived in a resort town called Pinawa. It was beautiful—right by the lake. There were deer everywhere, and they seemed so tame. It was hard to believe that people actually hunted the very same deer during hunting season out there. I had never been to a place like this before, and I loved every moment of it. Needless to say, Ted's family welcomed me with open arms. I felt like I belonged right away. While there, we went on many fishing adventures, as it seemed like everyone who lived there owned a boat of some kind. It was beautiful. Homes there were so much cheaper than back home. I seriously considered moving there, if it weren't for my children and my fiancé's work.

Once we got home we began to seriously look for homes we could afford. It was quite exciting, as it would be the first thing we owned together. When we did find the home we loved, we both had debts from our past, and not very much savings. My mum was kind enough to help us out. She gave us a loan, which helped toward the down payment. We appreciated that very much.

And once we moved in, it was finally time to make our marriage plans. I had romantic ideas of being on a beach barefoot, getting married in a traditional way in Hawaii. I also liked the idea of maybe being married on a ship. But neither was practical, especially as we were both just beginning our lives together in a new home. After discussing the possibility of a wedding of over one hundred people, we finally decided to keep it smaller, and agreed to get married in the pub where we had met—Finnegan's Wake.

We picked about fifty people to invite, including Ted's family—though unfortunately they were unable to come. We arranged with the pub to be married by a minister of our choice, on a Saturday when the pub was open to the public—since we knew so many people there, we thought it would be great. We'd get the wedding catered, but would not have to pay for the DJ, as the pub already had one—in fact, there was even a live band playing on that day. I was a thrifty shopper, and in the town there was a store called the Nearly New Shop. I found an Yves Saint Laurent tuxedo, brand-new, and paid twenty dollars for it. It was as if it had been tailored for Ted. On that very same day at another thrift shop, I found a beautiful wedding dress which still had its original tag on it: $1,000. I also paid twenty dollars for that one, and I did the alterations myself. It was all just falling into place so very nicely. I wondered when someone was going to wake me from the dream.

The day of the wedding was a rainy November day, but that didn't matter to me. My son was going to give me away. My very dear friend, May, was to be my maid of honor, and my daughter a bridesmaid. I was actually nervous—like it was my first marriage all over again. As my son walked me up to the minister (the pub tried their best to make it an aisle), I of course became quite emotional. But I was so very happy, and I knew that everyone there was very happy for me.

Today I was to become his wife, and I was so happy. The ceremony went so well. The pub had decorated the place for us. The funniest thing happened when I was to sign the registry after we were announced as husband and wife: I almost signed the wrong name, my ex-husband's. I quickly changed that, as I was so very happy to take Ted's last name.

We had a buffet, the bar was open to our guests, and the party began. I don't believe there is one photo from that day in which I was not smiling. It was one of the happiest days of my life—a happiness I never thought I would see in my life again. Many people who knew us, who happened to be at the pub that night, came up to congratulate us both. What a party it was. It was strange that after the wedding we went to our own home. And of course, once again, the question went through my head: *Do I deserve this?*

Our honeymoon was Ted's very first cruise. I had been on quite a few, but this time it was with someone I loved very much. Ted loved every moment of it.

The years have passed, and we're still together. People may wonder, have I been cured of my illness? Well of course not. But I continue to cope with it every single day. Thank goodness I have a supportive husband and family. Of course, I have my ups and downs—but thank God that Ted understands what I go through. I have learned to tell him if I am going through a bad spell. I have even learned to ask for a simple hug if I feel that might help. He is always there to give me what I need.

Sadly, a few years back, Ted lost his mother in a car accident. She was a wonderful woman, and during our last vacation with his family she and I had discussed having a day with just the two of us. Unfortunately, that never happened. A year later, his dad, who wasn't even ill at the time, passed away. I believe it was due to a broken heart. He was a wonderful man.

I can see where Ted's qualities come from. He is a combination of two special people who we miss very much: his mum and dad.

My friend May and I still keep in contact. I always remind myself of all she did for me. She is and always will be the angel who saved me from hell.

Sadly, I too have lost a very special person who was also my best friend: my sister, Paton. She suddenly passed away, alone in her apartment, of a cardiac arrest. I miss her terribly. Who would have thought, after all the times she was there for me, that she herself also suffered from mental illness and schizophrenia, only to die so suddenly and so alone? I miss her so very much. Paton had survived a quadruple bypass and her mental illness, and it saddens me to think of all she had gone through, with all the demons that she constantly suffered from in her head. She was strong not just for herself, but for me also, always. I think back to how Paton was always there for me when I was very ill—always supportive and loving. To see her suffer broke my heart.

Paton used to work at a hair salon, but was involved more with the spa aspect of the business. She had her own area of the salon, and was doing rather well. A short while after Paton's husband passed away from cancer, she became quite ill, because she came off her medication. When she came off her meds and became really ill, I didn't realize why it seemed so different compared with times she had done this in the past. I found out during one of our conversations prior to this that one of the people she worked with had given her ecstasy. I asked her why she did that and expressed how dangerous it was, but Paton was a very open-minded person. Although it may have seemed harmless to her, and although she felt that the people she worked with had no intention to mess with her and her meds this way, I felt very angry—not at her but at them. It seemed like they wanted to see what it would do to her in her mental state. They knew my sister had become very ill again, but thought it was funny to do this to her. After that, she became someone I didn't know, and it really scared me.

I could clearly see that there was something more wrong with her this time. I remember when I called her over and over again and got no answer. I became worried and decided to drive there after calling my niece, Paton's daughter, and my mum—asking if they had heard from her. When I found out that none of them had heard from her, I frantically jumped in my truck and searched everywhere I thought she might be. But I couldn't find her. I met up with my mum, and we decided to drive around the area again. For some reason, I told my mum to drive to the recreation center across from the building where Paton lived.

I remember shouting out suddenly, "Paton's there, Mum, she's there!" Paton was sitting on the curb outside of the recreation center, and did not look at all like my sister. My mum stopped the car, and I got out to talk to Paton, as everyone knew how close I was to her. Paton became very aggressive with me—to the point that I actually became scared. I kept trying to ask her to come with us, and she kept refusing. She got up and threatened to slap me. Paton's eyes were dark as coal—almost as though a demon was inside her. I started crying, because being so close to her and hearing her say that to me, I knew it was my sister talking. I can't really remember the details, but I do remember that she got home. That was all that we could do for her at this time. Paton had gone and thrown away almost everything in her home. If we even suggested taking her to the hospital, she would get very angry. She spoke about throwing almost everything she owned away, as though it was a normal thing to do. Where was my sister? Why was this happening to her? Paton didn't deserve this.

I believe it was a couple of days after this incident, Ted and I brought Paton to our home, because we wanted to take her out of her home. We wanted to create a diversion, because the only way we could help her at this point was to let the police know that she was a danger—not only to herself, but to others. When she saw the police car come, she knew what we had done and became very angry. We tried explaining to her that we were trying to help her. We could not get her to the hospital by asking her to go, so we had to take the next step, which was one of the hardest things for me to do. I felt like I was betraying her. That of course was not my intention. A policewoman came into our home, and in a very calm manner got Paton to go into the police car. I cried, as I thought that she would never ever forgive me. They then proceeded to take her to the hospital, where she was admitted.

I have to say this set off a lot of triggers for me, given my own illness. I remember having the police called on me when I was first married. Literally the "men in white coats" came to see if I was a danger to others or myself. I had to leave my home. My heart broke now knowing we had to do this for Paton—but I also knew it was the only way to get her the help she needed.

We were told that the ecstasy she had taken, combined with the medication in her system, had caused a part of her brain to have irreversible effects—she would have to live with this. I believe this is also when we were told that she was schizophrenic. When I went to visit her in the hospital lounge, the person standing there was not my sister—didn't even look like her. Her entire persona was dark. Talking with her was like talking to a stranger. She wanted change for the phone at the hospital, so I went through my purse to see what I could find. I held it out for her to take, and she just knocked it out of my hand. I didn't know how much longer I could stay there and see her like this. Sadly, I felt relieved when it was time to go. As we came down in the elevator once again, I cried for my sister Paton. She didn't deserve to go through this. I just wanted my sister back so badly it hurt.

How could this person I loved so much—who was there for me during my hard times, when I was in the hospital struggling with my mental illness—be in this situation? I never ever saw that coming. It was as though I had been hit by a bus and didn't know how to cope with it.

Paton was in the hospital for a while. I remember when she was doing better than when I had last seen her. I told her about how she almost slapped me, and she laughed, because she knew it was not like her to do that. She apologized. She didn't have to apologize—I mean, look what she was going through. She then told us that she actually felt she had the devil inside her during that time. Paton explained to us in detail what it was like. Sadly, even though she had experienced, what she felt was the devil inside her and that was over, she now heard voices in her head constantly. Paton explained how unbearable it could get at times, as the voices were always there, even if she told them to go away.

Once Paton was back home, she could not believe

that she had thrown out almost all her possessions. It was very sad. But she was assigned to a psychiatrist and a social worker who came to visit her regularly. She was on a series of medications. I knew how difficult it was to be put on a medication, as the doctors tried to find out what was best by trial and error. For her it was not a pleasant experience whatsoever. This medication honestly did change who she was, but at least she was no longer the person she had become prior to this. Now I could see that she was my sister—however, just by looking into her eyes, I could see how she was struggling. Paton would constantly speak of the voices in her head, and what they were saying to her. It was quite disturbing. I just could not imagine what she was going through.

I remember as time went by that they did change her medication. The new medication seemed to be better, but of course it was not a cure—it never is a cure for any of us with mental illness—but she was able to cope better. During family gatherings, she would suddenly get up and say, "Okay, I want to go home now." It would always be very unexpected, but she would almost get herself in a panic—she just had to leave, as she became overwhelmed. What it must have been like, I can't really say. But I know when you have a family gathering or are out anywhere where there are many people, it can become overwhelming, especially when you hear voices in your

The Darkness Within

head in addition to all the actual voices speaking in the room.

I will say this for Paton: she was a trooper. Paton had been through a lot in her life, and had overcome many hurdles. This, to her, was just another hurdle. She had to try and cope the best she could.

Because Paton was alone, and Ted and I were the closest to her in distance and in her heart, Ted would take her grocery shopping every Saturday. She loved his company, and it was better than me taking her, as I take my time when I go to the store. Ted and Paton preferred getting in and out quickly. She often took him for breakfast on these days, and always showed how much she appreciated the help. I remember her telling me before she passed away, "When it's your birthday, let me take you out to breakfast where Ted and I go." I really wish I had taken her up on her offer. Now she's gone, and there are so many things we still had to do together. I blame myself for not doing them with her.

I have many fond memories of the both of us singing out loud in my truck on the highway, waving to everyone driving by. She had a laugh and a smile that would make anyone happy. She may have been my older sister, but we were so very close, and used to have our private little jokes—the kind where we could just look at each other, and both know what the other was thinking, and burst out laughing. I really miss those days. All I have now is her photo in my home office. She had a beautiful smile, and was a beautiful person both inside and out. I have a small pewter urn with her ashes, which I had inscribed with the words "In My Heart"—and that is where she will always be.

Her loss really took a toll on me. I cannot deal with death like many other people. I cannot view a dead body to say my goodbyes. I'll never forget that day when Ted went to see if she was okay at home and found her. I could not believe and still don't believe that she is gone. I was affected the same way when my father passed away. He was only fifty-four years old. To this day it doesn't seem that long ago.

It's times like these when, once again, I question my faith. I can't understand why someone is taken from you so suddenly.

To this day, I still live with the guilt of when my dad passed away. I will tell you why. It all happened so fast. I didn't even know that my dad had a heart condition in his twenties, after World War II, during which he served in the British Army. We didn't even know that my dad had posttraumatic stress disorder, because back in those days nobody ever spoke of disorders or mental health. It was something many thought you had to be ashamed of.

Well I remember the day when my dad had to go for a stress test at the hospital. When I came back from work that night, I saw my mum sitting with him, and he was crying. When I asked what happened I was shocked to hear that basically my dad had a heart attack while doing the stress test. He was told that there was a ninety percent blockage of his arteries. To have surgery, especially back then in the late seventies, would mean a big risk—he could die on the operating table. He was also told that he had to stop work immediately. He had worked since he was a boy—he didn't even know the meaning of not working.

He became withdrawn, extremely weak, and very quiet. I didn't really understand what was happening to him. He had always been such a strong person. He loved music, and worked so hard. And now this happens? He could no longer enjoy the things that made him happy.

What made it even worse is that I was never really a favourite of either my mum or my dad. Paton was my dad's favourite, and my other sister was my mum's. One day prior to my dad having his stress test done, he and I were out to get something, and we got lost for over an hour. In that hour I became the closest I have ever been to my dad. We talked and talked—something we didn't often do. I do believe that getting lost that day was a blessing to me, as I saw the love my dad had for me that day. It was very special, something I will always remember.

Sadly, that happy moment was taken away from me, and once again I questioned my faith. Why was this happening to my dad? We'd only just become so close—it just didn't seem fair. I know it sounds selfish, and actually I guess it was, but I just felt like my dad was being taken from me. I have never dealt with loss or change very well.

As the weeks passed after my dad had been told what was happening to him, he became weaker. There were a few times he was hospitalized, and we thought right there and then we were going to lose him, but each time he came back home, so I felt there was still hope. The days he was hospitalized were stressful—every time the phone rang, we all jumped, thinking the worst.

Three months passed, and my dad had not spoken, and still I could not understand why. One morning before leaving for work, I didn't even kiss him goodbye, as I usually did. I just said bye, thinking he didn't want to talk to me—another selfish thought—and went to work.

At around 10:10 a.m., my boss took me into the conference room and told me that my dad had passed away that morning. Needless to say, I was in shock. They sent me home in a taxi. When I got home, I did not know how to deal with this. I kept thinking, *Where is my dad? He was here this morning, this cannot be happening.* My poor mum had been with my dad since she was thirteen years old, as her mother had died at a young age, and my mum had to play mother to her siblings. As she sobbed, she told us, "Daddy knew he was dying. He even folded his clothes neatly, put them on the bed and told me not to worry—that everything would be okay." Then she told us that he had an attack in the shower, and was pronounced dead when the coroner got to our home. That entire time was a blur to me. I was in disbelief, because I never did see my dad after that day—due to my fear of death, I didn't even go to the hospital to say goodbye to him.

To this day, I have lived with tremendous guilt, because I never said goodbye to my dad—at least not the way I should have. The morning he died I left angry, thinking that he just didn't want to talk to me—when he was actually preparing himself for death. I remember being in the funeral home. I had to stay outside, as my mum insisted on an open casket. I know my dad would not have wanted that, but I guess she really didn't know what to do. Because I could not deal with seeing anyone dead, or even being in a funeral home, I stayed outside of the room he was in. I put my hand to the wall, hoping he knew I was sorry, and that I loved him dearly. I sobbed.

When everyone came out of the room, I looked around at all these faces we hadn't seen in years—including my dad's brother—and said out loud, "Why are you all here? You were never there for my dad unless you wanted something. None of you visited him. So why come and see him now?" I became very angry—to the point where the funeral home director had someone take me out of the funeral home.

Sadly, Paton was not there for the funeral. At the time, she lived in England. She had just visited my dad, and it seemed that he had held on just long enough to see her. After she went back, it was like he just gave up. When everyone started coming out, I remember my mum holding my hand, and the hand of my other older sister, Jane, as though we were little girls again. We all walked to the car, just sobbing in disbelief. I remember how badly my mum cried—my dad was the only man she had ever been with and loved.

My anger remained with me when everyone came to our house after the funeral. I just could not face all these people who ostensibly cared for my dad, but who unfortunately never showed it when he was alive. I just went to my room and lay on the bed and cried myself to sleep. My dad was gone and I missed him and that tremendous guilt of not saying goodbye to him remained with me.

Death, as I have said before, is something I still have difficulty coming to terms with. I remember when we lived in England, I was sitting with my nana. I was seven years old. I began crying. When she asked me what was wrong, I explained to her that I was scared of dying. To this day it puzzles me why that would even cross my mind at that age.

When I think back to the deaths of my dad and Paton, I feel like part of my heart and soul went with them—something I would never get back. Now I worry about my mum passing, and that fear lingers—I feel I would not be able to handle yet another death in our family. Not that she is ill—but she *is* eighty. As I have always done, I worry about what might happen.

Because I still see a psychiatrist, I keep notes of how I have felt between appointments with her. For a long time after I was first hospitalized for my illness, I used to keep journals and write in them every day. I then started dictating my journals on mini-cassette tapes, but that all came to an end when I lived with the monster I spoke of earlier—somehow he got hold of my journals, and actually started transcribing them on his computer. Back then, I didn't know how to tell him he couldn't do that—it was personal, as I had to deal with the consequences.

Everything I have had to deal with over the years has left me with various triggers—they may occur due to a word, the smell of a certain type of alcohol, the environment of a hospital, or a touch by anyone—including a doctor. It's horrible to have this happen—especially when it happens out of the blue. However, I have learned to recognize the triggers now, and very often I tell Ted when I feel I have been triggered by a memory. Poor guy. Ted has had to deal with a lot during the years we have been married, as I have had several suicide attempts, due to things that have happened—not necessarily having to do with him, but how I was feeling at a particular time.

But don't get me wrong: I have come a long way since I was first diagnosed with clinical depression and post-traumatic stress disorder. My medication has not changed for many years. It seems like the doctors finally found the right cocktail to help me cope. I know there are many people who suffer from the same thing I have, and feel they can handle it without having to see a doctor or be on medication—but believe me when I say, if you need medication, then take the damned thing and stay on it. Don't feel you can come off it whenever you feel like it, because you will have to deal with the consequences, which will not be pleasant. You will hurt people you love.

It's strange—here I am, an adult dealing with mental illness, taking my medication, seeing my psychiatrist when I should. But I still feel I am living with my demons when I come across people—yes, adults—who like to bully, especially on social media. Yes, I was bullied as a child, but believe it or not there are adults in this life of ours who feel it necessary to continue this bizarre behaviour.

I, like millions of others, have used Facebook and was able to reach out to family members, to post memories, and to do so many other things. It was my connection to the outside world, but in the safety of my own home—or so I thought. I joined a group there—we all met through a karaoke app which

I subscribe to (I find singing is great therapy—a way of expressing myself). Anyway, I joined this group on social media, as I was invited by the admin and thought it might be fun. Many of them were from England. It was a private group, and some of the things people did on there were quite inappropriate. Why I didn't leave the group is beyond me—I guess I felt it was a way of making some friends, something I find very hard to do due to trust issues from a young age.

Just before Paton passed away, I was having a horrific time in this group. Three grown women started to pick on me quite openly in this group—it got somewhat out of hand. I decided I wanted to leave, and the next thing I knew, there was slander about me all over social media, including on this particular platform. People were saying disgusting things about me, and about Ted—they said he was a child molester, which of course was the worst thing they could say. I did as the site suggested—reported all sixty-two people and the group, and blocked them all. I couldn't deal with it. I was still dealing with it the day I found out Paton had passed away. How can people be this way? I don't understand it, yet *I* am the one with the mental health issue? Anyway, after all the damage they did—including causing me to become suicidal again before I found out how to deal with them, and having them try to destroy my family—I ended communication with all of them.

I think going through that made me somewhat

stronger, strangely enough. I found it gave me the strength to stand up for myself and put an end to these people's relentless behavior. Shortly after Paton passed away, somehow I got the strength to create my own group on this social media platform. It was also a private group, but one to help others like myself, who might be dealing with illness or other kinds of stress. I met these people on the same karaoke app, and they all became family to me. The group ran very smoothly, and it gave me a sense of pride, as I honestly felt I had created a safe place for these people to express themselves—in song, or words, or any other format. I even had several people tell me that I had helped them—that was the best thing I could have been told, as in the past, it had usually been other people helping *me*.

I had to use my husband's account to let my group know that my Facebook account had been compromised and that the only way I could be on there at the moment was with Ted's account—they knew he was also part of my group. What's sad is that since having my account deleted, so many people have left the group. I feel like I have let them down. I feel absolutely lost, sad, and a failure. I haven't seen my psychiatrist in a couple of months, and haven't talked to her about this, but really feel I have to, because it has affected me very much. I cannot take the isolation.

One of the reasons I cannot handle it is because

of one of the medications I have been on since 1996, Clonazepam. It causes me to have short-term memory loss. If I stay on it, it will cause long-term memory loss and other serious side effects. My psychiatrist is weaning me off this extremely slowly, as it is a dangerous drug to just stop. It will be a while until I can actually come right off of it. It's also causing me anxiety to the point where I don't want to leave my home. Not that I am afraid to leave my home—I just get anxious at the thought of doing so. I only get out for doctor's and dentist's appointments, and the odd family gathering. I have a 2017 jeep in my garage, which only has 950 kilometers on it, and now it's February 2018. What's wrong with me? I did raise this issue with my psychiatrist, and she is concerned—however, we're at a bit of a standstill at the moment with that particular issue.

So with me not getting out of the house, then having my Facebook account disabled, I feel absolutely isolated and have days where I cannot handle it. Ted works from home two days a week, just so that I have him home with me, which does make me feel better. It's strange how social media can have such a hold one you, but it can—I do believe that the people who run Facebook feel they can control people's lives, because they obviously do all the time and don't care about the consequences of their actions. This is strictly my personal opinion.

One of the problems of feeling isolated—I should

add that I'm not one to pick up a phone and call someone either—is that it gives me a lot of time to think. That isn't always good. Prior to this all happening, I have had bad things go through my head, out of the blue when I least expected it. I have had to literally tell myself out loud to stop it. No, I'm not hearing voices like my sister—just thoughts which sometimes involve my family members being in an accident or worse. I have no idea why these things come to mind out of the blue—it takes me back to when I was seven, when I said I was scared to die. I mean, where did that come from?

The mind is a strange thing. Everything I have been through causes me to really try and understand why things happen the way they do. I wish I had more education—I think I would have loved to learn more about how our brain functions and how we can change the way we think. I don't know if I would ever have made a good psychiatrist—I can't imagine listening all day every day to people's troubles. I do think I would have made a good therapist, though, as I know I have helped many people in my past, regardless of my illness, by listening and offering advice when needed. I know it takes far more than that, but I do believe I could have done a good job. Who knows—maybe in my next life.

When I really think about it, I don't give myself enough credit, as I have overcome many obstacles in my life. Sure, they haunt me at times, but I have been learning how to cope with them and speak out about them. I also know I have many more obstacles to face. But I am here. All of those suicide attempts? Yes, they happened, but I always got something back from each time. I have learned a lot about myself, and every day I learn a little bit more. I still have to learn how to forgive myself for things I regret in the past—but that takes time. I know it my heart that I have been forgiven. I have accepted who I am and what I have been through. And I hope to be able to help others overcome their demons.

ABOUT *the* AUTHOR

Michele Gmitrowski was born in Calcutta, India, but raised in the United Kingdom from the age of four. When she was sixteen, she and her family immigrated to Canada, where she still lives today. Her heritage is a mixture of Spanish, Irish, Armenian, and British.

As a child, Ms. Gmitrowski was a tomboy—always playing soldiers with the neighborhood kids, and loving to write detective stories as a pastime. As she grew older, she became a lover of poems, and eventually had one of her own published in 2004, in *VoicesNet Anthology*.

After high school, Ms. Gmitrowski started working in Toronto as an executive assistant for a major bank. She stayed there from 1977 to 1996, until she had to go on permanent disability for mental health reasons.

Michele Gmitrowski

Ms. Gmitrowski is now happily married, and has two wonderful children from a previous marriage (a son and a daughter), as well as two grandchildren, and a third on the way. Her family makes her feel quite blessed.

www.ingramcontent.com/pod-product-compliance
Lightning Source LLC
Chambersburg PA
CBHW072207100526
44589CB00015B/2417